GROWING GODLY

A Woman's Workshop on Bible Women

Books in this series—

After God's Heart:
  A Woman's Workshop on 1 Samuel
  by Myrna Alexander

Behold Your God:
  A Woman's Workshop on the Attributes of God
  by Myrna Alexander

Growing Godly:
  A Woman's Workshop on Bible Women
  by Diane Brummel Bloem

New Life:
  A Woman's Workshop on Salvation
  by Carolyn Nystrom

Our Life Together:
  A Woman's Workshop on Fellowship
  by Lawrence O. Richards

Walking in Wisdom:
  A Woman's Workshop on Ecclesiastes
  by Barbara Bush

A Woman's Workshop on the Beatitudes
  by Diane Brummel Bloem

A Woman's Workshop on Bible Marriages
  by Diane B. and Robert C. Bloem

A Woman's Workshop on David and His Psalms
  by Carolyn Nystrom

A Woman's Workshop on Faith
  by Martha Hook

A Woman's Workshop on Forgiveness
  by Kirkie Morrissey

A Woman's Workshop on James
  by Carolyn Nystrom and Margaret Fromer

A Woman's Workshop on Mastering Motherhood
  by Barbara Bush

A Woman's Workshop on Philippians
  by Paul and Margaret Fromer

A Woman's Workshop on Proverbs
  by Diane Brummel Bloem

A Woman's Workshop on Romans
  by Carolyn Nystrom

GROWING GODLY

A Woman's Workshop on Bible Women

Student's Manual

Diane Brummel Bloem

Lamplighter Books Grand Rapids, Michigan
Zondervan Publishing House

Unless otherwise indicated, all Scripture passages are quoted from The New International Version, Copyright © 1978 by The New York Bible Society.

GROWING GODLY: A WOMAN'S WORKSHOP ON BIBLE WOMEN—STUDENT'S MANUAL
Copyright © 1983 by The Zondervan Corporation
Grand Rapids, Michigan

Edited by Evelyn Bence and Julie Ackerman Link

Printed in the United States of America

84 85 86 87 88 89 90 / 10 9 8 7 6 5 4 3 2

My sister,
Arlene R. Brummel Rhoda,
kindled my interest in the women
of the Bible. Through the years
she has shared her thoughts with
me and fanned the flame of my
interest and enthusiasm by giving
me books and articles on this subject.
I dedicate this book to her with
thanks and love.

CONTENTS

ACKNOWLEDGMENTS

I thank my friend, my critic, my sounding board, my beloved husband, Robert C. Bloem, for his help and encouragement in the writing of this book.

I thank Evelyn Bence and Julie Ackerman Link for their perceptive suggestions and skills in the editing of this book.

I thank my former teacher, Rev. Leonard Greenway, Th.M., Th.D., for his encouragement, suggestions, support, and for reading and evaluating this manuscript.

I thank the Lord for all He has taught me in this study and I praise Him for the blessings He will give to those who use this book to stimulate and guide their Bible study.

HOW TO USE THIS BOOK

To get the most out of any Bible study, one must be thoroughly prepared. This workbook contains questions that will help you understand the setting of the lives of biblical women and also questions that will make you think about what the Lord is teaching you for your life.

Before you attempt to answer any of the questions, read all the scriptural passages listed at the beginning of the lesson. You will want to answer each question before your group meets for discussion. You may take one or two questions a day as part of your personal quiet time or you may answer them all at one sitting. I think it best to take one or two questions at a time, thinking them over throughout the day. Ask the Holy Spirit to guide you in your study.

Throughout the writing of this book I have prayed earnestly that the Holy Spirit would enable me to compose questions that provoke thought, discussion, and sharing, so that each person studying the material will be spiritually enriched. The Lord began answering these prayers by teaching me. I know that if you study and participate in discussion, you will be blessed and others will be blessed through you.

INTRODUCTION

Name as many kinds of flowers as you can. Think of spring, summer, fall, and winter flowers; think of houseplants, garden plants, desert flowers, tropical flowers, flowers that grow in sun or shade, flowers that grow in clusters or single blossoms, flowers with fine, clinging stems or strong stalks; think of large flowers, tiny flowers, wildflowers, cultivated flowers, flowers on bushes, flowers on trees—the list could go on and on.

God has created flowers and plants in an infinite variety—all of them beautiful. God has also created an infinite variety of persons—each with a unique beauty. All are made so that God, the Creator, will be recognized and praised.

So often we judge others harshly because they are not like us. We fail to see their unique beauty and God's purpose for them in the world. In working and studying with women, I have come to appreciate their individuality and every day I see how God uses their beauty of heart, soul, mind, character, and body for His purpose and glory. I have come to see God's created beauty in myself and I marvel at it. I look forward to meeting an infinite variety of people from all races and nationalities when I get to heaven.

Women mentioned in the Bible are also beautifully unique. Sometimes we judge them harshly, but a study of their circumstances often changes our opinion of them. We see how God shaped them, pruned them, or transplanted them. We see their beauty and recognize that they were much like women living today. God teaches us to know ourselves and to trust His plan for us as we study His work in the lives of these women who lived so long ago.

God's Garden of Women is the theme of these lessons. Our first objective is to see the beauty of each of these Bible women, their environment, the circumstances that shaped them, the sins that blighted them, their stages of growth. We will see how God, the Gardener, worked in their lives.

Our second goal or objective is to recognize our own personal setting, stage of growth, blights, and beauties. We will see how God works in our lives.

A third objective is to become aware and appreciative of the beauty of others and to become understanding of their circumstances and struggles as God works out His purposes for their lives.

Binding all these objectives together is our chief goal, so that we might bring praise to God and trust His work as Chief Gardener.

To help us achieve these objectives we will try to compare each Bible woman we study to a flower, giving reasons why she is like that flower. Each lesson is introduced with some of my thoughts about the woman, comparing her to a flower, and the last question of each lesson asks the group members to compare the woman studied to a flower. I have done this with many women's groups and have found it a most effective device in summarizing all of our thoughts. After doing this, some women say they are reminded of that Bible woman every time they see that flower; they recall how God worked in her life.

Introduction

At the end of each lesson, I also encourage each student to think of at least one other person and of herself as a flower in God's garden. This may be done privately or expressed in the group discussion. At the end of the series, each person should be more understanding of and appreciative of others and more aware of her own beauty. This should result in praise for our God as Creator and Provider.

1

DINAH

Genesis 34:1–35:9

Forget-me-nots are welcome and lovely in my spring garden. Their seedlings, however, turn up everywhere and can become almost as troublesome as weeds. Some of them even grow in the grass and are cut down by the mower.

I think of these flowers when I study Dinah. After ten sons, Jacob's family must have joyfully welcomed her birth. Yet when she strayed from her home "garden," she brought grief and destruction to many. We never hear of her after the tragic account in Genesis 34, but we should not forget her and all that we learn from her life.

1. Where did Jacob and his family live at the time of Dinah's story (33:18)?

   Find this city on a map.

2. Where was he going (31:3, 13)?

3. What did Jacob do when he got to Shechem (33:19)?

   What was the significance of this act?

4. Had he arrived at the destination God had planned for him (Gen. 28:13–15; 20–22)? Use a map to trace his journey from Paddan Aram (northeast of Palestine).

Genesis 34

5. Why do you suppose Dinah wanted to go to Shechem (v. 1)?

6. What prompts young people, raised in Christian homes, to leave home and live in secular settings? Is the state of the parents' spiritual health ever a factor in the children's desire to leave the Christian community? Explain.

7. Dinah was raped. Was she in any way responsible for this? Are women today morally responsible to protect themselves from possible rape or is this society's responsibility? Explain.

8. Did Shechem's subsequent love for Dinah and his desire to marry her right his wrong? Explain.

9. How was Hamor's plan (vv. 8–10) a deception of the Devil in the battle against God's kingdom (Gen. 3:15; Matt. 4:1–11; 2 Cor. 6:14–18)?

10. a. Did Dinah's brothers show a true dedication to God's covenant sign and promise when they suggested mass circumcision (vv. 13–17)? Explain.

    b. Was God pleased with this evangelical farce? (See Rom. 2:28–29.)

11. Is forced baptism or Christianizing good for Christ's kingdom? Explain.

12. What was Shechem's true motive? Hamor's? Simeon's and Levi's? (See vv. 19–29.)

13. What was Jacob's chief worry (v. 30)?

14. Did Shechem's sin justify a massacre? Why or why not? Consult Genesis 49:5–7 and Deuteronomy 22:28–29.

15. Discuss whether or not any of these actions were an expression of true love and concern for Dinah.

16. Describe situations where we are apt to guard our social reputations and concentrate on our personal hurts, neglecting the victims of sin or crime.

Genesis 35:1–9
17. What is the significance of God's command to Jacob in verse 1?

18. What was Jacob's response?

19. How was this great tragedy used for the spiritual welfare of Jacob and his family?

20. Describe one or more instances in which God has used personal tragedy to bring about greater commitment and rich spiritual blessings for His people.

21. When we thoughtlessly or willfully sin and cause great sorrow to ourselves and others, how can the following verses comfort us: Psalms 138:8; 139:23–24; Romans 8:28; Titus 2:11–14?

22. What flower do you think Dinah resembles?

2

MIRIAM

Exodus 2:1–10; 15:20–21; Numbers 12; 20:1; Micah 6:4

One morning I opened the kitchen curtains and looked out at my garden. What I saw made me sad. The stem of one of my beautiful tuber begonias had been bent and broken and the flower head hung there limply wilting. I broke it off and put it in a glass of water on the windowsill, wanting to preserve its strong, dramatic beauty. It had been a focal point in the garden, but now the broken stalk would never produce another flower. How could this have happened? Should I have supported that heavy flower head with some stakes?

When we study Miriam, we see her beautiful, dramatic role in the saving of God's people. The sad part comes in Numbers 12 and we ask, How could this have happened to Miriam? Can it happen to me?

Exodus 2:1–10

1. What can we learn about Miriam from her role in Moses' rescue?

2. Aaron was three years old when Moses was born (Exod. 7:7), so Miriam was their older sister. What are typical big-sister attitudes toward younger brothers? Give at least two answers.

3. Moses was brought up in the king's palace, tried to help his people, went into exile, became a shepherd, and was married (Exod. 2:10–21). What was Miriam's life like during that time (v. 23)?

4. Read Exodus 4:27–31. Imagine yourself as Miriam and tell how you would have felt at that time about your brothers and your future life.

Exodus 15:20–21

5. Miriam is here called a prophetess. What does that mean?

6. What might be the significance of her being called Aaron's sister, not Moses' sister?

7. What can we learn about Miriam from her actions here? (See also Micah 6:4.)

Numbers 12

8. We don't know much about Moses' wife mentioned here. Some say she was black, an Ethiopian, and Moses' second wife. Others claim this was Zipporah, who had rejoined him (Exod. 4:18–26; 18:1–6), and that she was not a true believer or a proper help to Moses. Why do you suppose Miriam and Aaron opposed Moses because of her? Consider 1 Corinthians 7:32–35.

9. Did they complain directly to Moses? Who heard them? How did the Lord feel about this?

10. Was their complaint really against Moses and his wife or was something else troubling them? What?

11. Can you think of any time when you have exploded over a trivial matter because some other problem had built up anger in you? How should you handle such problems?

12. How was God's relationship with and call to Moses different from His relationship with and call to Aaron and Miriam (Exod. 3:10; 4:27; Num. 12:6–8)?

13. Why did Miriam receive the more severe punishment?

14. How do Aaron's words and tone in Numbers 12:11–12 differ from those in verse 2?

15. How did Moses respond?

16. We do not read of Miriam again until her death (Num. 20:1). What, if any, leadership role do you think Miriam played after her leprosy was cured?

17. Read Psalm 75:6–7; Matthew 20:26–28. Do these verses imply that we should not seek advancement or recognition? What about campaigning for church or political office (1 Tim. 3:1)? Does a title or recognition make work more meaningful?

18. How can internal power struggles harm the church?

19. What guidance for talented and gifted Christian leaders can be found in 1 Peter 3:8 and Philippians 2:1–5?

20. How can you support, encourage, and restore Christian leaders who suffer temptations or pitfalls as Miriam did?

21. Of what flower does Miriam remind you?

3

RAHAB

Joshua 2 and 6; Hebrews 11:31; James 2:25

Loosestrife is the strange name given to some beautiful wildflowers that wave like scarlet and purple ribbons in marshy roadside areas. One August I transplanted a clump of them. With faithful watering they have adapted to my garden and the spikes of loosestrife stand tall and beautiful and brave alongside the marigolds and petunias.

When I see these scarlet flowers, I often think of the scarlet cord Rahab put in her window before she was rescued and transplanted into the nation of Israel. She was brave and she became a source of blessing for the whole world.

1. Read Joshua 1:10–11. As we begin this study, what is about to happen?

Joshua 2

2. Rahab is called a harlot or a prostitute. Why might the godly spies have gone to her for lodging?

3. Why would Rahab have wanted to protect foreign spies (vv. 6–9)?

4. Discuss whether or not it was right for her to lie to protect them. (See also James 2:25–26.)

5. What shows that Rahab had faith in the true God?

6. What prompted her to believe?

7. What can we learn about Rahab's character and personality from verses 12–16?

8. What does the scarlet cord symbolize (Exod. 12:7, 13; Rom. 3:23–26; 1 Peter 1:18, 19)?

9. What significance is there in Rahab's whole family being saved because of her faith? (See also Acts 16:31–34; 1 Cor. 7:12–16.)

10. God used the faith of Rahab and her report of the fears of her people to encourage the spies. They were then confident that the Lord was about to fulfill His promises to His people (v. 24). How can conversions or demonstrations of faith encourage people today?

11. In the genealogy of Jesus given in Matthew 1, only four women are mentioned besides Mary: Tamar (v. 3—see Gen. 38), Rahab (v. 5), Ruth (v. 5), and Bathsheba (v. 6—see 2 Sam. 11). All except Bathsheba were not born into Israel and all except Ruth were associated with adultery. What significance do you find in these facts?

12. Rahab is called "the harlot (prostitute)" throughout the Bible. Does this justify keeping the memory of people's sins alive in our conversation, for example, "So and so—the one who cheated on taxes, the one who had a baby out of wedlock . . ."?

13. Rahab was the mother of Ruth's second husband, Boaz (Matt. 1:5). How do you suppose Rahab treated her daughter-in-law, the Moabitess?

14. Discuss whether or not Rahab and her family would be welcome in your church.

15. Rahab and Sarah are the only women mentioned by name in Hebrews 11 (vv. 11 and 31). What distinguishes Rahab?

16. What kind of flower will remind you of Rahab?

4

DEBORAH AND JAEL

Judges 4:1–5:15

Deborah does not remind me of a flower—she reminds me of a tree. Perhaps this is because a tree is mentioned in the narrative.

We have twenty oak trees on our small lot and they fascinate me. Besides producing countless acorns to feed the squirrels and countless leaves to shade us in summer and keep us busy raking in autumn, they have amazing defense mechanisms. When insects attack the embryo acorns, the tree builds an apple-like gall around the insect to keep it from harming the tree. These galls become additional food for squirrels. When storms come, oaks seldom snap, but bend and sway in the wind with incredible grace. They endure.

Isaiah 61:3 says, "They will be called oaks of righteousness, a planting of the LORD for the display of his splendor." Deborah may have dispensed justice under a palm tree, but to me she represents an oak of righteousness.

Jael reminds me of the English hawthorn, a small, attractive tree that promises shelter, but possesses dangerous thorns. Legend tells us the plant was used as a sedative. Jael sedated Sisera so she could kill him when he came to her for shelter.

1. Read Judges 2:6–23. Summarize the spiritual condition of the Israelites at this time. How did the Lord plan to use the nations to bring His people back to true worship?

2. How well equipped were these foreign armies (Judg. 1:19; 4:3)?

3. How well was Israel equipped (Judg. 5:8)?

4. What may we infer about Lappidoth? Is it significant that Deborah was a wife and mother (Judg. 4:4; 5:7)? Explain.

5. What is a prophetess (Judg. 4:4–7; Exod. 4:12, 16; 7:1–2; Jer. 1:7; Ezek. 3:4)?

6. How did Deborah get the authority to judge the people, commission a general, and raise an army? (See Deut. 16:18–20; Judg. 2:18; 4:5.)

7. Why might Barak have wanted Deborah to go along with him (Judg. 4:8; Ps. 108:11–13)?

8. What do we learn about Barak from Judges 4:8–9, 14?

9. What is significant about Deborah not personally leading the armies into battle, as did Joan of Arc?

10. If possible, study a map and find the territories of Naphtali, Zebulun, Issachar, Ephraim, and Benjamin. Find Mount Tabor and the Plain of Jezreel. Note the topography (mountains, plains, valleys). What armies are stationed in which types of areas? How would fighting in hills and mountains differ from fighting in plains?

11. How did the Lord give Barak and his troops the victory (5:4–5, 19–21)?

12. What was Jael's family background? Why did Sisera feel safe in her tent (Judg. 1:16; 4:11, 17–18)?

13. Why do you suppose Jael killed Sisera (Judg. 4:20–21; 5:24–27)?

14. What is the tone of Judges 5? Compare it with Psalm 68, especially verses 1–3. Who receives praise in this song?

15. What spiritual truths can be learned from Deborah's song?

16. Why does Barak get the credit in Hebrews 11:32?

17. What does this study of Deborah and Jael teach us about women's roles in the home, church, or politics?

18. Of what flower does Deborah remind you? Why?

19. Of what flower does Jael remind you? Why?

5

NAOMI AND RUTH

The Book of Ruth

I don't know how it got there, but one morning I looked out and saw a new flower in my garden. Small white rosettes grew on a tall slender stalk next to the blue balloon flower. As I was admiring its delicate beauty, my neighbor said, "There's a weed in your garden," and pointed to the newcomer.

"A weed?" I asked.

"Yes, there are thousands of those growing in the field near the creek."

"This isn't a weed," I said. "It's a wildflower that has found a home in my garden. It looks lovely with the blue balloon flower. See how they lean on each other, almost intertwining. They hold each other up."

I thought about that for a day or two and now when I look out and see my unidentified wildflower, I call it Ruth, and its blue companion, Naomi.

1. When does the story of Naomi and Ruth take place (1:1)?

2. What do we know about Moab and its people? (See Gen. 19:36–37; Deut. 2:9; 23:3–6; Judg. 11:14–18; 1 Sam. 22:3–4; Isa. 16:2–5.)

3. Discuss whether or not it was right for Naomi and Elimelech to take their young sons to live in a pagan land? What does their decision say about their trust in God?

4. Discuss what considerations contemporary believers must make before deciding whether or not they should move away from a Christian environment to better themselves economically?

5. What can we learn about Naomi from Ruth 1:6–14? List at least three things.

6. What motivated Ruth to want to go with Naomi (1: 16–17)?

7. How had Naomi's grief affected her (1:19–21)?

8. In Old Testament times what provision did God make for widows (Deut. 24:17–22; 25:5–6; Ps. 68:5–6a)?

9. How did God provide for widows in New Testament times (Acts 6:1; 9:39; 1 Tim. 5:3–16; James 1:27)?

10. Does the Christian community, as you know it, effectively care for widows? Explain.

11. What can we learn from Ruth 2:6, 10–13 about how strangers are often treated? Search for phrases that infer negative and positive reactions to Ruth.

12. What difficulties do newcomers or new converts or immigrants often experience in long-established churches? How can these difficulties be avoided or overcome?

13. Was it right for Naomi and Ruth to conspire to trap Boaz into marriage by compromising his and Ruth's reputations (Deut. 25:5-10; Ruth 3)?

14. How does a believer know when to wait things out and when to work things out?

15. What can you learn from this study about the qualities that produce a good relationship between mothers-in-law and daughters-in-law?

16. If you look at this story as a drama, who is the director and main character? (Ruth 1:6, 8, 13, 17, 20, 21; 2:12, 20; 3:10; 4:11-12, 14)?

17. Why might God have planned for Ruth to be an ancestress of Jesus (Matt. 1:5, 16; Isa. 16:5)?

18. In view of Ruth 4:14–17, do you think Naomi's name was once again fitting—"pleasant" instead of "bitter"? Explain.

19. How can God use grandchildren to minister to grandparents?

    What special blessings can children receive from their grandparents?

20. Of what flowers do Ruth and Naomi remind you?

6

HANNAH

1 Samuel 1:1–2:36

I finally found a spot where I believed a rosebush could live happily and productively. It was on the far side of the house beneath a bedroom window. It would get sunshine part of each day so I planted it and watched for results. It grew, but it produced no flowers. I got more joy out of visiting a neighbor's prolific rosebushes.

One day I noticed that my bush had one bud which began to unfold into a fragrant, velvety-red flower. I picked that first flower and took it into the house so I could enjoy it all day.

Hannah reminds me of that rosebush.

1. What do we learn from 1 Samuel 1:3–4 about the family's spiritual commitment?

2. What do we learn from 1 Samuel 1:5–8 about this marriage?

3. How is this marriage with its joys and griefs comparable to situations of divorce and remarriage today?

4. How intense was Hannah's feeling in this longing for a child and why?

5. Discuss whether or not Hannah should have been satisfied to have only the love of her husband.

6. In what ways might women who have children increase the pain of those who want children but don't have any? How should they help one another?

7. Why did Eli think Hannah was drunk? What can we learn from Hannah's response to his unjust accusations?

8. Why would Hannah promise to give her child back to the Lord at an early age?

9. Study Hannah's prayer (1:1) and her response to Eli (1:15–18). Find at least three indicators of Hannah's spiritual state, her faith, and commitment. What can Hannah's prayer teach us?

10. Hannah is the first person in the Bible to address God as "LORD of hosts" or "God of armies" or "LORD Almighty." Why do you suppose she used this name for God?

11. When Hannah brought Samuel to the tabernacle, did she place him in a good environment (2:12–36)?

12. What joys or sorrows might Hannah have experienced in giving Samuel up at such a young age?

13. If your child told you that he or she had decided to become a missionary in a foreign field, what would your response be?

14. Should all long-awaited or "miracle" children be urged to go into special kingdom service?

15. How did God further bless Hannah (2:18–21)?

16. a. Hannah was given two to four years to train Samuel. How would you change your priorities in child training if you knew the child would be under your influence for such a short time?

    b. How does this lesson speak to the trend of mothers of babies and young children working outside the home?

17. What enabled Hannah to pray so joyfully and trium-
    phantly when she gave up Samuel?

18. Of what flower does Hannah remind you?

7

MICHAL

1 Samuel 18:20–30; 19:8–17; 25:39–44;
2 Samuel 3:12–16; 6:16–23

Michal makes me think of the day lilies in my garden. I'm so pleased when they open, giving bright, cheerful color to our shady plot. When they close, however, they are anything but beautiful. The long petals droop and pucker together making them look like a withered banana peel. I hurry to snap them off and throw them away, never letting them form a seed pod. Similarly, Michal played an important, colorful part in David's life, but after she bloomed, she withered—showing ugliness—and was never allowed to produce seed.

1 Samuel 18:12–30

1. Why was Saul pleased that his daughter Michal loved David?

2. Why was David reluctant to become Saul's son-in-law?

3. Saul's son (18:3) and daughter (18:20) loved David. Judah and Israel loved David (18:16). God loved David (18:14). Why did this make Saul afraid, and an enemy of David?

1 Samuel 19:8–17

4. Why did Michal lie to her father's men?

5. Why did she answer her father as she did (19:17)?

1 Samuel 25:39–44

6. What happened to Michal while David was fleeing from Saul?

7. How might Michal have felt about these events in her life?

8. Considering the facts recorded in 2 Samuel 2:8–11, what was Michal's status or position?

2 Samuel 3:12–16

9. Why did David want Michal back when he had other wives (2 Sam. 3:2–5)?

2 Samuel 6:1–23

10. What do you learn about David in verses 1–19?

11. Why did Michal despise David and fail to share his spiritual enthusiasm?

12. What was David's response? Do you agree with him?

13. How do believers today inhibit one another's spiritual expression?

14. Does God regard such squelching as sin? Explain.

15. Discuss whether or not David should have tempered his exuberance because of the sadness in Michal's life. Should he have been more dignified?

16. What should our response be when people who once brought us pleasure or helped us bring us pain and inhibit the expression of our spiritual experiences? For guidance, consider this matter from David's and Michal's viewpoints and discuss how God can use such trials for a believer's spiritual growth. Consult Psalms 28 and 36.

17. God promised the kingdom to David and his descendants forever (2 Sam. 7:12–16). How did Michal play a part in the fulfillment of this prophecy?

18. What flower is Michal like?

8

THE SAMARITAN WOMAN

John 4:1–42

Our shady yard is brightened by beds of multicolored impatiens. One July day I walked past our round garden and noticed a bright pink impatiens plant that had a drooping head and leaves. I thought, Can it be that dry? I'd better water it. Looking around I saw that all the other impatiens needed watering too.

Because of Jesus' statement to the Samaritan woman about living water, I began thinking of her as that pink impatiens plant, growing in the shade, apart from the others. Because I saw its need for water, all the others got the drink they needed. Many Samaritans were given living water because one of them, isolated from the others, went out to draw water one day and met Jesus.

1. In Mideastern countries it is customary for the women to draw water in the morning and evening—it is almost a

social event. What may we infer from the fact that this woman came to the well alone at noon?

2. Most pious Jews traveling from Judea to Galilee took a circuitous route, crossing to the other side of the Jordan River to avoid going through Samaria. Why does verse 4 say, "Now he had to go through Samaria"?

3. Who were the Samaritans (2 Kings 17:6, 24–34, 41)?

4. How did their religion differ from the Jewish faith (2 Kings 17:33, 41; John 4:12, 20, 25)?

5. Why did these ethnic and religious differences make the Jews hate the Samaritans? Note the ridicule in the Jews' words to Jesus in John 8:48.

6. What is the significance of water, which Jesus used to represent salvation? What did He mean by living water?

7. Jesus exposed this woman as an adulteress. How did Jesus deal with adultery? (See also Matt. 5:27–32; John 8:3–11).

8. Today there is widespread condoning of adultery, pre-marital sex, and couples living together without marriage. What should be the Christian's attitude toward those who are practicing such sins?

9. When Jesus exposed the Samaritan's sin (v. 18), why did she begin discussing a proper place of worship (v. 20)?

10. Describe other ploys used by people confronted with the gospel. How should we deal with this problem?

11. Jesus told her plainly that He was the promised Messiah (vv. 25–26), although He did not speak this clearly to others. Why?

12. What do you notice about her response (vv. 28–29)?

13. Jesus broke many traditions in speaking with her (v. 27). What can we learn from this?

14. Why was this woman's witness so effective (vv. 29–30, 39)?

15. Do you think these people became true believers (vv. 40–42)? Why or why not?

16. How did the Samaritans receive the apostles after Jesus' death (Acts 8:4–17)?

17. What have you learned from this study that will make you a more effective Christian witness?

18. What kind of flower was this Samaritan woman?

9

MARY AND MARTHA

Luke 10:38–42; John 11:1–12:9

I have a friend who grows beautiful African violets on the windowsill above her kitchen sink. I remarked about this once because I had always thought of geraniums as kitchen plants and African violets as belonging on a living room table. But who's to say? Why can't violets be in the kitchen and geraniums brighten the living room?

Whenever I think of Martha and Mary, I see them as a geranium with bright, bold flower and strong stalk, and an African violet—soft, delicate, shyly hiding blossoms in plush leaves. Each has a role of beauty in the house, but that role is not restricted to a certain room. Houseplants and sisters are movable and can bloom, side by side, as they follow the Light.

1. Mary, Martha, and their brother, Lazarus, lived in Bethany. What do we learn from reading John 11:5, 18; Mark 11:11; Matthew 21:17; and Luke 24:50–51?

2. Briefly describe Mary and Martha.

Luke 10:38–42
3. What was Martha's complaint?

4. What should Martha have been doing? Serving or sitting at Jesus' feet? What was her real problem?

5. Did Jesus tell Martha to become like Mary? Explain.

6. What is the good part which Mary chose?

7. What can we learn from Jesus' way of rebuking Martha?

8. If you had to choose between going to Bible study or preparing a good meal for guests, which would you choose? Which *should* you choose?

9. When feeding our family or guests, how can we balance the time and effort put into food preparation with that put into fellowship and worship?

10. Who showed greater faith when Lazarus died, Mary or Martha (John 11:17–43)? Explain.

11. Why did Mary anoint Jesus (John 12:3; Mark 14:3–9)?

12. Is this anointing the same as the one recorded in Luke 7:36–50? Why or why not?

13. How can we show our love to Jesus as Mary did?

14. How can we show our love to Jesus as Martha did?

15. Can a person be too much like Mary and not enough like Martha? What would be the ideal?

16. What flowers remind you of Mary and Martha?

10

SALOME

*Matthew 20:20–28 (compare with Mark 10:35–45);
27:55–56; Mark 15:40–41; 16:1–8*

We buy a lot of sunflower seed. Our children like to eat the kernels and we like to feed wild birds. Sunflowers have strong, tall stalks. Their heavy flower heads turn and follow the sun. Sometimes their heads droop.

I think Salome was a sunflower. She was strong; she helped provide food for Jesus and His followers; through her children, generations of people have been fed spiritual food. She followed the Sun of Righteousness. Her head drooped when Jesus rebuked her and when she witnessed His death, but she knew the great joy of believing in the resurrected Lord as her Savior and she loved to serve Him. I hope to meet her in heaven.

1. Who was Salome's husband (Matt. 4:21; 27:56; Mark 15:40)? What do we learn about this couple from Mark 1:19–20; 15:40–41?

2. What do we know about their sons, James and John? (You may read about them in Matt. 4:21–22; Mark 3:13–17; 5:37; 9:2; 13:3; 14:32–33; Luke 9:51–56; John 19:26–27; 20:2–10; 21:1–3, 20–25; Acts 1:13; 3:11; 4:3, 13, 18–23; 12:1–3; Gal. 2:9; Rev. 1:9–11ff.)

3. Compare the names listed in Matthew 27:56, Mark 15:40, and John 19:25. Many Bible students believe that Mary the wife of Clopas is the same as the mother of James and Joses. Since it is unlikely that two sisters would be named Mary, it is thought that Jesus' mother's sister (John 19:25) is Salome. She would then be Jesus' aunt and James and John, His cousins. Note that John points out this relationship and assumes responsibility for the care of Jesus' mother (John 19:25–27). How would this explain Salome's, James's, and John's involvement in Jesus' ministry and their request in Matthew 20:20–28 and Mark 10:35–45.

4. What was Jesus teaching in Matthew 18:1–5; 19:30?

5. How did the disciples interpret Matthew 19:27–29?

6. What had Jesus told the Twelve just before Salome, prompted by James and John, came with her request (Matt. 20:17–19)?

7. How was her request made (Matt. 20:20)?

8. Why was this request made? How might Jesus' words in Matthew 16:17–19 have prompted it?

9. Should we ask the Lord for honors for our children? Explain.

10. Can greatness be achieved through humility? Give examples.

11. Does humility require us to ignore our talents and belittle ourselves? Explain.

12. What is the tone of Jesus' reply in Matthew 20:21–23?

13. Do you think the disciples understood and accepted Jesus' words in verses 24–28? Explain.

14. What key word derived from verse 28 describes the Christian's path to greatness?

15. How can we teach our children to serve Christ and others joyfully and willingly?

16. Since Salome followed Jesus to the cross and to the tomb, how do you think she took Jesus' answer to her question?

17. Do you think Salome was active in the early church (Acts 1:6–14; 2:1–4, 42–47)? Explain.

18. Was Salome's request for honor for her children granted? How? Did she and they drink of the cup of the Lord's suffering?

19. What has the Holy Spirit taught you in this lesson?

20. What kind of flower is Salome?

11

MARY MAGDALENE

Luke 8:2–3; Mark 15:40–47; Luke 23:55–56; Mark 16:1–3; John 20:1–18

When I go to the grocery store at Eastertime, the fragrance of hyacinths draws me to the display of potted plants. Hyacinths have sturdy stalks, beautiful flowers and that pungent fragrance that sends the excitement of new life and spring surging through me.

When I think of Mary Magdalene, I think of her love for Jesus poured out in the spices she carried to the tomb on Easter morning. Mary, healed, was a strong individual; she loved Jesus with her whole being. She was the first person to see the risen Lord and to triumphantly proclaim the good news to others. She was a fragrant Christian, a hyacinth. "But thanks be to God, who always leads us in triumphal procession in Christ and through us spreads everywhere the fragrance of the knowledge of him" (2 Cor. 2:14).

1. In *Webster's New Collegiate Dictionary* (1979, p. 684) we find the following item:

mag-da-len or mag-da-lene *n. often cap.* [Mary *Magda-len* or *Magdalene* woman healed by Jesus of evil spirits (Luke 8:2), considered identical with a reformed prosti-tute (Luke 7:36–50)] 1: a reformed prostitute   2: a house of refuge or reformatory for prostitutes.

Read Luke 7:36–50, 8:2–3; John 12:1–3. Do you be-lieve that these passages teach that Mary Magdalene was a reformed prostitute as history has depicted her? Ex-plain.

2. Mary was from Magadan or Magdala, a city on the west-ern shore of the Sea of Galilee. We are told that Jesus cast seven demons out of her. Demons seem to have been very active in the years of Jesus' ministry, especially in Galilee where He did a lot of teaching and healing (Matt. 4:23–24; Mark 1:21–28; Luke 8:26–38). Why do you suppose this was true?

3. While not calling them demons, we know that people today may be controlled by certain sins. Name some of these sins (Gal. 5:19–21). How can the power of Christ heal and help someone overcome them?

4. After reading Luke 11:24, tell what a person who has been freed from the control of drugs, alcohol, or other sins should do to keep from being "repossessed."

5. How did Mary show her thankfulness for healing (Luke 8:3; Mark 15:40–41)?

6. Although many other women also followed and helped Jesus, Mary Magdalene is listed first in Matthew 27:56, 61; 28:1; Mark 15:40, 47; 16:1; Luke 24:10; and John 20:1. What does this suggest?

7. Try to reconstruct the events of Easter morning from the accounts in Luke 24:1–12 and John 20:1–18.

8. Why did Jesus tell Mary not to hold on to Him (John 20:17)?

9. Why did Jesus want her to tell the brethren that He was returning to the Father?

10. Contrast Mary's words in John 20:13 with those in verse 18.

11. What parts of Psalm 30 would express Mary's feelings?

12. What was Mary's testimony (John 20:18)?

13. Why is her witness important to us (1 Cor. 15:17–19)?

14. As a believer in Christ's resurrection and ascension, how is your life different from the life of an unbeliever?

15. What flower is like Mary Magdalene?

12

LYDIA

Acts 16:11–15, 40; Philippians 1:1–10

When I was a little girl, I would sometimes pick one of my mother's lavender irises and wear it as an orchid. To me it was more beautiful than any expensive orchid from a florist's shop.

I have great difficulty in thinking of Lydia without thinking of purple, one of my favorite colors. She seems to have been wealthy, charming, and gracious—somehow striking like a lovely orchid. Yet, since she met Paul at the riverside, I see her as an exquisite purple water iris, her roots going deep into the living water.

1. Read Acts 16:6–10. Paul wanted to continue preaching in Asia, but the Spirit sent him to Europe. How did Paul and his companions respond to this call?

Acts 16:11–15, 40

2. Where was Philippi? What do we know about the city (v. 12)?

3. List at least three things you learn from verse 13.

4. What do you learn about Lydia in verse 14?

5. Name two women who were fellow believers with Lydia (Phil. 4:2–3).

6. How did Lydia translate her belief into action (v. 15)?

7. Lydia was a Christian career woman. How can Christian commitment be expressed in a woman's career?

8. Lydia was also a homemaker. How did she use this position for the Lord? What can contemporary women learn from Lydia as they struggle to balance homemaking and careers?

9. What do the following passages teach us about Christian hospitality: Romans 12:13; Hebrews 13:2; 1 Peter 4:9; 1 Timothy 3:2; Matthew 10:42; 25:42–46?

10. What can you learn about the Philippian church from Philippians 1:1–9; 2:19–30; 4:14–16?

11. Paul wrote this epistle from a prison cell, probably in Rome. What did he pray for the Philippian Christians (Phil. 1:9–11)?

12. What did these church members face and how were they to face it (Phil. 1:27–30)?

13. What comfort or challenge given to Lydia and her friends in Philippians 4:4–20 is God giving to you through this study?

14. To what flower would you liken Lydia?

13

LOIS AND EUNICE

Acts 16:1–5; 2 Timothy 1:1–5; 3:14–15

Episcias are related to African violets. We have three flourishing episcia plants on our living room table. Their bright, red, trumpet-shaped flowers brighten the room all year long. These plants send out runners that produce rosettes of leaves and flowers. These can be used as cuttings to propagate the plant. My first episcia was given to me by my sister-in-law Dorothy. My other two plants are the daughter and granddaughter of that original one. I have given cuttings to many people who now enjoy the flowers and share them with others.

I think of Lois as a grandmother episcia plant whose spiritual beauty was passed on through Eunice to Timothy, to many early Christians, and eventually to us.

1. What do we learn about Timothy's mother, Eunice, from Acts 16:1?

2. Can faith be passed on as a gift from parents to children?

3. What spiritual riches are enjoyed by persons whose ancestors are true believers?

2 Timothy 3:14–15

4. When did Timothy's spiritual training begin?

5. How can we teach the Scriptures to children under two?

6. Paul tells Timothy to continue in what he has learned because he knows those from whom he learned it. Why is it important that we know our teachers?

7. What did people say about Timothy as a boy (1 Tim. 1:18; 4:14)?

8. What did people say about Timothy as a young man (Acts 16:2)?

9. How do their peers often regard young people who are committed to serving the Lord?

10. How should Christian parents respond to these attitudes of their children's peers?

11. Discuss whether or not parents and grandparents should urge young people to choose careers in full-time Christian service.

12. Why did Paul call Timothy his son (1 Tim. 1:2, 18; 2 Tim. 1:2; Phil. 2:22)?

13. What can we learn about Timothy from Philippians 2:19–24?

14. What do we learn about Timothy in 1 Timothy 5:23 and Hebrews 13:23?

15. What can Christian parents do to help when their grown children go through severe trials?

16. How can believing grandparents spiritually nurture their grandchildren?

17. Do Christian heritage and training in themselves qualify a person for eternal life? Explain.

18. May Christian parents take the credit when their children turn out good?

19. What spiritual heirlooms can parents leave for their children and grandchildren? Name specific values and characteristics. Point out their importance in life or give examples of your appreciation of the values you inherited from your parents and grandparents.

20. What flowers remind you of Lois and Eunice?